A Hip Hop guide to punctuation

Dennis M Keating
The Honolulu Guy

www.HonoluluGuy.com

Featuring the Artwork of James Ishizaki AKA Jimmy Sparrow

Dennis M Keating

Books by Dennis M Keating

The Olympics:
An Unauthorized Unsanctioned History
*

Charlie Whitman
Was a Friend of Mine
*

Ena Road
*

The Fulda Gap
*

A Chicago Tale
*

Black Lahu
*

Poetry for Men
*

The PUNCTS

Dennis M Keating

The PUNCTS

We're The PUNCTS.

We're the Grammar Gang.

Mess with us,

and it's Ram, Bam Clang.

DEDICATION

To all the students & future students of the world, especially:

Patrick, Demetrius, Sophie,
Claire, Jason, Colin, William,
Abdullah, Asiya, Amina, Saya,
Summer, Sophia, Lila, Blake,
Hao Yu, Zhi Lin,
Tommy, Nick, Alyssa,
Finn, Trinity, Tristan,
Malachi, Asher
and Quigley

Let's make learning
a fun thing.

ACKNOWLEDGEMENTS

My Mentor
Professor Steven Taylor Goldsberry

Artist
James Ishizaki
AKA Jimmy Sparrow

Proofreader – Faith Scheideman

My Wife and Proponent – Sandy

The PUNCTS book and The PUNCTS song were written by
Dennis M Keating
AKA
The Honolulu Guy
www.HonoluluGuy.com

PUBLISHED BY
GOLDEN SPHERE

ISBN-13: 978-1-63538-023-1

DENNIS M KEATING OWNS ALL RIGHTS TO THE MATERIAL, LYRICS, POETRY AND ARTWORK IN THIS BOOK. FOR INFORMATION, USAGE RIGHTS OR FOR ANY OTHER REASON PLEASE CONTACT HIM AT:
LOSTPUKA@GMAIL.COM
OR AT: DENNIS M KEATING
 P.O. BOX 75100,
HONOULU, HI 96836, USA.
Copyright © 2017 Dennis M Keating
All rights reserved.

The PUNCTS

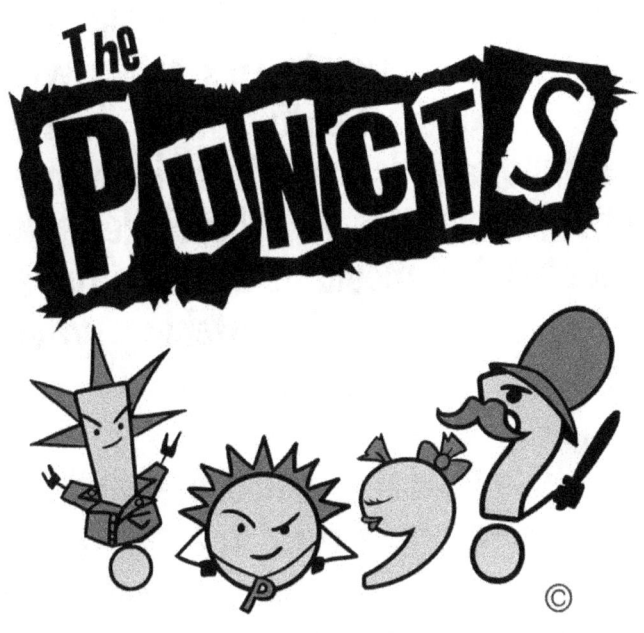

Introduction

The author of The PUNCTS, Dennis M Keating, believes learning should be a fun thing. He wrote this books with this in mind." Keating, who lives in Waikiki, and is sometimes known as The Honolulu Guy, believes learning punctuation should be as much fun as going to the beach, catching waves and getting some rays.

In the old days, dinosaurs and old English teachers ruled the earth; and there were fourteen punctuation marks. Then, computers, the internet and email changed our methods of communication. Today, Facebook and Twitter are replacing formal letters, postage stamps and envelopes. With this, the punctuation marks we use and their number is also changing. In this book, we show nineteen punctuation marks. We believe this number will change in the future.

Come on in. Welcome to our turf, meet our Gang and become our friend.

We're The PUNCTS.

Dennis M Keating

Cast of Characters
in order of Appearance

Period

Question Mark

Exclamation Point

Interrobang

The PUNCTS

Quotation Marks

Apostrophe

Ellipsis

The PUNCTS

The PUNCTS

PERIOD

PERIOD is our popular
go-to guy.

Sure, he's plain and small,
but he's very spry.

Often, he's the last one
to leave the scene,

Wrapping things up,
All neat and clean.

The PUNCTS

A PERIOD is primarily used at the end of a simple sentence. A simple sentence usually offers information or states facts.

PERIODS are also used in initials, abbreviations, titles, dates and acronyms.

In addition, **PERIODS** are often seen in computer language and mathematics.

The PUNCTS

We're the PUNCTS.

Come join our show.

And in a short time,

you'll be a grammar Pro.

QUESTION MARK

**QUESTION MARK is
like a downtown Cop**

**Easy to see;
tall and roundish on top.**

**Give him the scoop,
straight and fair,**

**When he comes asking
Who? What? Or Where?**

The PUNCTS

A QUESTION MARK is used when you ask a question.

When you are uncertain about something or need information, you usually ask a question.

Teachers may ask questions to see whether the students understand the lessons or if they are awake.

The PUNCTS

We're the PUNCTS.

Do you want an "A"?

Then listen up

And do what we say.

EXCLAMATION POINT

**EXCLAMATION POINT is
a party-hard kind of guy.**

**He thrives on excitement
and getting high.**

**He's a crazy rocker who
blasts round the clock**

**Too much of him, and your
fans will be in shock.**

The PUNCTS

27

EXCLAMATION POINTS are like shouting, so use them sparingly. You should save **EXCLAMATION POINTS** for rare, special occasions. No one likes people to scream in their ears. Well, maybe it's O.K. at a rock concert.

This said, with the advent of social media, teens seem to use **EXCLAMATION POINTS** more frequently to get across their messages. Maybe, teens have been to too many rock concerts; or maybe, they live more exciting than their English teachers.

We're the PUNCTS.

Just follow our dictate,

Otherwise, you'll

Never graduate.

INTERROBANG

**INTERROBANG is the Big
Bad Berserker of our lot.**

**When things get too crazy,
he's what we got.**

**Bringing confusion and
shock along his way.**

**This wild & crazy guy
was born in the USA!**

The PUNCTS

An INTERROBANG fuses together an EXCLAMATION POINT with a QUESTION MARK. An INTERROBANG is used to indicate excitement, shock, and/or disbelief. It can be a used in a rhetorical question of surprise, like when your mother says, "You did what‽"

The PUNCTS

We're the PUNCTS.

We make the rules.

Do as we say,

Don't be no fools.

COMMA

**COMMA is cute and curvy,
and a wee bit sassy,**

**She likes action, and can
make your prose classy.**

**With a shapely figure
That will make you pause;**

**It's no surprise, her curves
Can stop a clause.**

The PUNCTS

Normally, COMMAS separate parts of a sentence, such as two clauses. Also, they are used to separate items in a list.

COMMAS look similar to APOSTROPHES. However, COMMAS like PERIODS are at the baseline of the text, while APOSTROPHES hover near the top.

The PUNCTS

We're the PUNCTS.

We make the laws.

Follow our style

and you won't have flaws.

COLON

COLON is a funny, juggler kind of guy,

He can balance periods two on high.

He's a clever trickster who doesn't use a prop,

Then, right in mid act, he brings things to a stop.

The PUNCTS

A COLON precedes a quote, a list or an explanation. When using a COLON, you should have two considerations. First, a COLON needs to be preceded by a sentence or an independent clause. Second, if you were to use the word, "namely" rather than the COLON, your sentence would still make sense.

COLONS are also used for Bible verses, as in. John 2:5; for ratios, as in 3:1; and for stating hours and minutes, as in 10:45 AM.

The PUNCTS

We're the PUNCTS.

Just follow our code.

If you do this,

You'll be on the right road.

SEMICOLON

SEMICOLON has fun playing two on one.

For her, a clause on each side is double fun

She's tempting, alluring and an eager guide;

Whispering, "Let's be a threesome, one of you on each side."

The PUNCTS

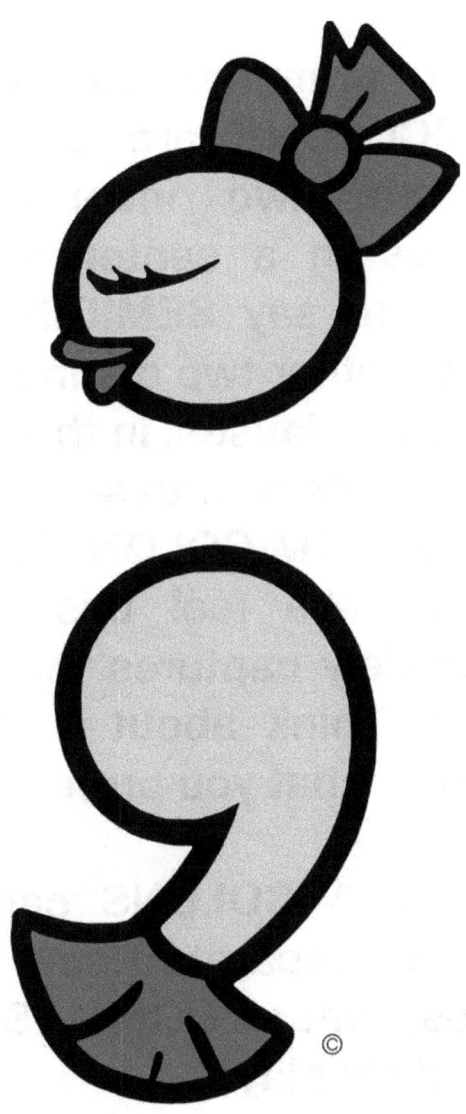

Often, grammar books say SEMICOLONS are used to separate two independent clauses in a sentence. We prefer to say SEMICOLONS join together two distinct and separate clauses. In this way, they create a threesome that has a SEMICOLON in the middle. We feel this more accurately captures the final result. Think about it. Then choose what you prefer.

Also, SEMICOLONS can be used to separate items in a series, where COMMAS are already in play.

The PUNCTS

We're the PUNCTS.

Want to make your teacher happy?

Then, do what we say,

and do it real snappy.

AMPERSAND

**This Dude, AMPERSAND
is 2,000 years old.**

**Despite his age
he's active and bold.**

**He's pop with teens,
cause he's fast and neat;**

**They hang with him
on both Facebook or Tweet.**

The PUNCTS

The AMPERSAND has roots that go back to the Romans in the first century A.D. long before English became the Lingua Franca of the world.

The AMPERSAND simply means "and." It is commonly used in business names and abbreviations. It is also used in programming language. Recently, for brevity, it has found popular usage in social media.

The PUNCTS

We're the PUNCTS.

We control the game.

Join with us,

and you'll have no shame.

QUOTATION MARKS

QUOTATION MARKS are Gossip gals traveling as a pair;

When someone's chatting, these chicks are right there.

They're inverted twins, together since birth,

Just perk up your ear; they'll give you the dirt.

The PUNCTS

QUOTATION MARKS always come in pairs. They indicate you have chosen to repeat what someone else already said, word for word.

QUOTATION MARKS can also be used to indicate you consider the word inside the marks to be a slang word or an inappropriate word.

The PUNCTS

We're the PUNCTS.

We may sound rough,

But if you listen up,

You'll have the right stuff.

APOSTROPHE

APOSTROPHE is a lady of contraction and possession,

She makes letters disappear in every session.

She can chew up letters body and soul.

She's a power chick; and an earthly black hole.

The PUNCTS

An **APOSTROPHE** often indicates one or more letters have been eliminated, as when "do not" becomes "don't."

APOSTROPHES can also be used to show possession. In this instance, it shows who the item belongs to: "That's Laila's hat."

The PUNCTS

We're the PUNCTS.

Is joining us, your dream?

Then just learn our signs,

And you'll make the team.

ELLIPSIS

**Mystery cloaks ELLIPSIS
with her . . . mark.**

**She whispers to her lovers
and leaves them dangling in
the dark.**

**"Dear, . . . I love you . . ."
when strolling in the park;**

**Is she sincere, or just out on
a lark?**

The PUNCTS

An **ELLIPSIS** looks like this: . . . and consists of three dots or periods in a row.

An **ELLISIS** indicates some words have been eliminated. Usually, an author would use an **ELLESIS** because she/he considers these words to be superfluous.

The plural of **ELLIPSIS** is **ELLIPSES**.

The PUNCTS

We're the PUNCTS.

Don't make no Bad,

Or Your English teacher

Will be plenty mad.

HYPHEN

HYPHEN is the peace keeper of our herd,

She can unite strangers and form a new word.

She also gives aid to injured terms that ache

By rejoining syllables torn by a line break.

The PUNCTS

HYPHENS join two unrelated words and create a new word with the hyphen placed between the two old words. Over time, as the new word becomes popular, its two parts meld together and poof, the **HYPHEN** disappears. It's just like band aids disappear when cuts heals.

Also, a **HYPHEN** is used when a word is too long for a line. Then, the word is broken at a syllable and a hyphen is inserted near the end of the line and the remaining letters are put on the next line.

The PUNCTS

We're the PUNCTS.

Just follow us, and you'll pass.

And who knows?

You may rise to the top of the class.

DASH

Is DASH a space surfer or riding an airboat?

Whatever! He can hop into sentences and start to float.

Being a polished actor, he can play several roles.

Causing a dramatic pause is often among his goals.

The PUNCTS

A **DASH** can have several uses. While a **DASH** may look like a minus sign or **HYPHEN**, it's different and has different uses. The most common is to set off some information for emphasis. **DASHES** are also used to set off a quote.

DASHES are like **COLONS** – they're less formal, but cooler.

A **DASH** can indicate "from and too" as in "Read pages 51 – 79." Also, it can replace the word "and" as in "2012 – 2013."

The PUNCTS

We're the PUNCTS.

Just follow our line;

And, in English class,

You're sure to shine.

SLASH

**SLASH sounds like a Zorro
type of guy,**

**He may appear forward, but
he's really geeky and shy.**

**He hides in HTML links,
dates and other things.**

**And snuggles so close,
you might say he clings.**

The PUNCTS

The **SLASH** is rarely seen in formal writing. But hey! who writes anything formal, these days? That said, you can find **SLASHES** in poetry where they indicate line breaks.

A **SLASH** can also be used:
in fractions: 4/5;
in dates: 12/25/2018;
and as a substitute for "per" as in: 85 miles/hour.

In addition, some computer languages use **SLASH** is also used in some computer languages.

The PUNCTS

We're the PUNCTS.

Now, how about that?

Join up with us

and be a real cool cat.

BACKSLASH

BACKSLASH leans backward and seems a bit slow.

You won't see him much, in most places you go,

Except when you enter computer land.

There, his name can change with a software brand.

The PUNCTS

Commonly, you'll only see **BACKSLASH** in computer land. As his name implies, he's is a backward **SLASH** or a mirror image of **SLASH**.

BACKSLASH is another Born In The USA guy. He came to life with computers and hippies in the early 1960's.

BACKSLASH has been given several different names by computer geeks. These names include: hack, whack, downwhack, bash, slosh, backwhack, reverse slash, reverse slant, and backslant.

The PUNCTS

We're the PUNCTS.

We control the scene.

Hang with us,

And things won't get mean.

BRACKETS

BRACKETS often hold comments within their grip.

Often, this info isn't necessary for the script.

His straight hard sides make his face look like a square.

Some authors feel his comments are akin to hot air.

The PUNCTS

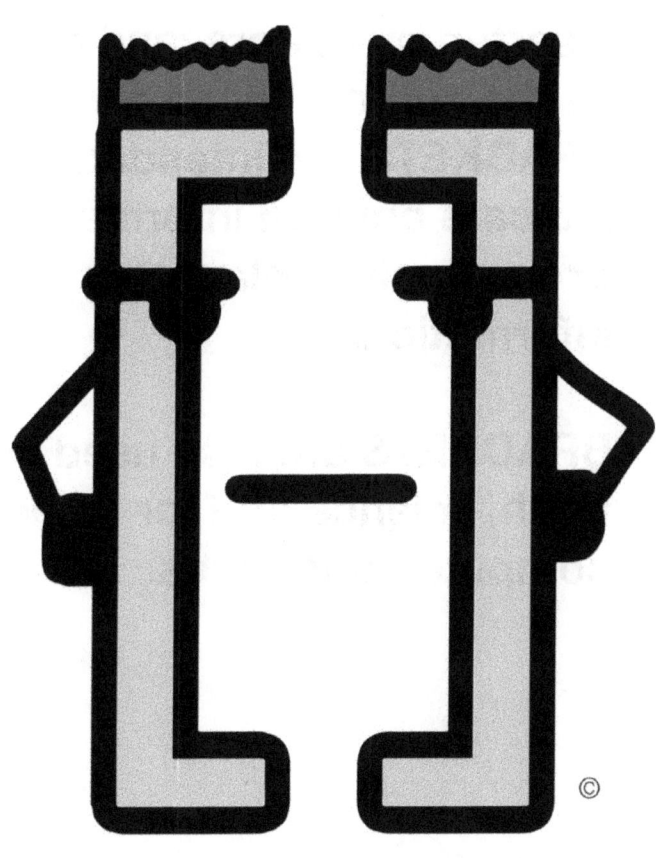

Usually, BRACKETS are inserted by editors, and not by the authors themselves. BRACKETS are intended to indicate omitted information or to supply explanatory information.

BRACKETS are also used in math, science and for some computer languages.

The PUNCTS

We're the PUNCTS.

Following us, is the key.

Do this, and you'll get

more than a "B."

PARENTHESES

PARENTHESES are rounded brackets, who come in pairs,

Asides and whispers are their main fares.

Providing unique information is among their joys.

To some artists, they are like bowlegged cowboys.

The PUNCTS

PARENTHESES provide extra information or supplemental information that may clarify a point or be beneficial to the reader.

Parentheses are also used for in computer languages and math.

Parentheses always come in pairs with the plural spelled parenthesis.

We're the PUNCTS.

we know the score.

Join us, and you'll learn

what friends are for.

BRACES

BRACES are shapeshifted brackets. Isn't that cool?

Their shape relates to a guideline rule.

They have an artsyfartsy design with a curly style.

For geeks, musicians and poets they bring a warm smile.

The PUNCTS

BRACES are also known as curly brackets. While **BRACES** are used in computer languages, they are most notably seen in poetry and music.

The PUNCTS

We're the PUNCTS.

we're the grammar crowd

March with us

and you'll be walking proud.

ANGLE BRACKETS

**ANGLE BRACKETS may
leave you agape**

**because of their
arrow like shape**

**For emails, math and physics
they remain cool**

**Other than that, they're
rarely seen in school.**

The PUNCTS

ANGLE BRACKETS are also known as chevrons. They are normally used to enclose highlighted material.

While **ANGLE BRACKETS** are uncommon, they are often found in math related topics and computer programming.

We're the PUNCTS.

We're the grammar kings.

Fly with us and you'll be royalty with wings.

ABOUT THE AUTHOR

Dennis M Keating, also known as the **Honolulu Guy**, is a lover of life, a teacher, a businessman, an entrepreneur, and a poet. He has taught PhD candidates, business managers, undergraduate and graduate students in Thailand, Great Britain, Mexico, Germany, China and the USA.

He enjoys a peripatetic lifestyle and has spent 40 years of his life outside of the continental USA.

For the last ten years, Keating and his wife, Sandy, have lived a quiet life in the bustling Waikiki neighborhood of Honolulu. He is often found pounding his iMac keyboard; hiking the Diamond Head trail, or strolling with his wife at sunset along the sands of Waikiki.

Keating has written a variety of books on diverse topics. His books relate to his multifarious interests and his personal experiences. You can view his books on Amazon or check Keating out on his website:

www.HonoluluGuy.com

Or his Facebook page:

https://www.facebook.com/
TheHonoluluGuy/

ALOHA

The Honolulu Guy

Who's your favorite member of the PUNCTS? Let us know on Facebook.

https://www.facebook.com/TheHonoluluGuy/

www.HonoluluGuy.com

www.ingramcontent.com/pod-product-compliance
Lightning Source LLC
Chambersburg PA
CBHW071312060426
42444CB00034B/1960